EMERGENCY!

BOMB DISPOSAL UNITS

DISARMING DEADLY EXPLOSIVES

by Justin Petersen

CAPSTONE PRESS
a capstone imprint

Edge Books are published by Capstone Press,
1710 Roe Crest Drive, North Mankato, Minnesota 56003
www.mycapstone.com

LIBRARY OF CONGRESS CATALOGING-IN-PUBLICATION DATA
Names: Petersen, Justin.
Title: Bomb disposal units : disarming deadly explosives / by Justin Petersen.
Description: North Mankato : Capstone Press, 2016. | Series: Edge books.
    Emergency! | Audience: Grade 4 to 6.? | Includes bibliographical
    references and index.
Identifiers: LCCN 2015034887 | ISBN 9781491480281 (library binding) | ISBN
    9781491484159 (ebook pdf)
Subjects: LCSH: Bomb squads—Juvenile literature. | First responders—
    Juvenile literature.
Classification: LCC HV8080.B65 P48 2016 | DDC 363.325/16—dc23
LC record available at http://lccn.loc.gov/2015034887

EDITORIAL CREDITS
Erin Butler, editor; Nicole Ramsay, designer; Sara Radka, media researcher

PHOTO CREDITS
freetextures: Texture18 cement, 2–32; Newscom.com: Joshua Sudock/ZUMA
Press, cover, Eddie Moore/ZUMA Press, 5, LARRY W. SMITH/EPA, 7,
The Washington Times/ZUMA Press, 9, PHC JOHNNY BIVERA/KRT, 10,
11, MATTHEW CAVANAUGH/EPA, 13, Tony Overman/MCT, 14, Haris
Memija Xinhua News Agency, 14, GHULAMULLAH HABIBI/EPA, 17, TIM
CHAPMAN/KRT, 19, Chris Maddaloni/CQ Roll Call, 21, Ken McGagh/
ZUMA Press, 22, CJ GUNTHER/EPA, 24, Orange County Register/ZUMA
Press, 27, James Vellacott/The Daily Mirror, 29

Printed in the United States of America in Mankato, Minnesota.
042016   009728R

TABLE OF CONTENTS

LIVES ON THE LINE

The phone at the police department rings mid-morning. Someone has threatened to set off a bomb in a busy office building downtown. Panicked, the employees called their local police department for help. This is a job for the department's bomb disposal unit. The team members gather their courage and spring into action.

At first the squad is unsure whether there is really a bomb in the building. The team members search the area with bomb-sniffing dogs. The dogs soon lead the team to a trash can holding a small bomb. The space is small, so the bomb technicians decide to use a robot to **defuse** the bomb. After working on the bomb from a distance, they finally defuse it. The office building is safe.

Bomb squads are made up of specialists who put themselves in danger to locate and disable bombs. Whether they are part of a police department or in the military, these technicians work hard to keep people safe. They are constantly finding new ways to protect people from deadly explosives.

defuse—to remove the part of an explosive that makes it explode

Bomb squads use specialized robots to help clear explosive devices while technicians stay at a safe distance.

Chapter 1

TRAINING FOR THE JOB

Becoming a bomb technician is no easy job. Applicants must first figure out if it is the right job for them. A bomb technician must be able to work calmly under pressure and feel ready to face dangerous situations on a daily basis. Other important skills include being a good **observer**, figuring out how things work, and working well on a team.

The next step is to start a career in either law enforcement or the military. Future police officers complete the police academy and then join a police department. After five years of experience, an officer can be considered for bomb squad training.

Bomb technicians in the military must first go through basic training. Then they go through specialized training for locating and dismantling bombs. Each branch of the military has its own training program for Explosive Ordnance Disposal.

observer—someone who pays close attention to the details of a situation or to his or her surroundings

Bomb squad trainees undergo many training exercises, using different scenarios, to help prepare them for real emergency situations.

GOING TO SCHOOL

Police officers and military personnel go through different training processes. A police officer can be accepted into training based on skill level and recommendations from the department. After being accepted into a training program, a future bomb technician must complete classes and tests. The amount of training depends on the requirements of the local team and on the technician's level of expertise. Training can last from two weeks to eight months.

State and local bomb technicians train at the Federal Bureau of Investigation (FBI) Hazardous Devices School in Huntsville, Alabama. This is the only school in the country that trains and **certifies** bomb technicians. At the school, trainees learn safe methods of defusing bombs. They also learn laws and regulations related to explosives and how to use safety equipment to protect themselves. They practice simulations of emergency bomb calls to put their skills to use.

Trainees also learn how to work as part of a team. They must be good communicators to work efficiently in an emergency.

During training students re-create explosions to learn how they can affect people and the surroundings.

certify—to officially recognize a person's abilities and skills

Training at the Hazardous Devices School

Leaders at the FBI's Hazardous Devices School know that bombs are a real
threat, and they come in many different forms. Training is made as realistic
and varied as possible for students. This means that practice scenarios are
based on real-life incidents that have occurred. One scenario simulates a
bomb that has been wired with explosives. Another mimics the emergency of a
bomb on the subway. The leaders make sure that students can learn and make
mistakes without the risk of harm. Still, they show students what would
happen if the mistake were made in a real emergency.

EOD training includes education on explosive military weapons and how to dismantle and dispose of them safely.

FACT:

A bomb suit weighs about 90 pounds (41 kilograms). Completing normal bomb squad tasks while wearing one of these suits is often part of training.

EOD TRAINING

The training process is different for bomb technicians in the U.S. military. Each branch in the military has a program called Explosive Ordnance Disposal (EOD) Training. The length of the program is different for each military branch.

EOD training is an intense and challenging program. It combines physical fitness with academic learning about bombs. The difficult training causes some trainees to drop out. In the four branches of service, 42 percent of trainees drop out of the program each year.

Once trainees complete the basic course, military bomb technicians begin on-the-job field training. After 18 to 24 months, trainees are issued the Basic EOD Badge, which is sometimes called the "crab." The "crab" has three levels. EOD technicians can earn the Senior EOD Badge after 3 to 5 years. The Master EOD Badge is awarded after 7 to 15 years.

Bomb-sniffing dogs also go through training.

Chapter 2

EMERGENCY RESPONSE

A call to the bomb squad normally goes through the police department first. The call is transferred to the special bomb squad unit. The bomb squad's first job is to sweep the area and find any bombs that might be there. To stay safe, the team members wear protective bomb suits and may use x-ray machines to investigate suspicious objects.

In the beginning stages, information is one of the bomb squad's most valuable weapons. Squad members often depend on the people who made the emergency call and other witnesses to provide information. These people can often provide details about the bomb threat, if they received one. They can also point out anything that looks out of place or abnormal in the area.

One of the best ways to locate a bomb is to use bomb-sniffing dogs. Dog handlers manage these **K-9s** on the scene and allow them to sweep the area. Thanks to their excellent sense of smell, dogs can locate bombs better than humans can.

K-9–a dog trained in special skills and used by an official organization such as a bomb squad or police force

Bomb squads rely on their canine teammates to smell and locate explosive devices.

FACT:
Not all calls to the bomb squad mean there is a live bomb. Only about one in five calls leads to a live bomb.

Bomb squads are called on to safely identify, remove, and destroy old explosives.

IEDs are often intended to look like harmless, everyday items, but they need to be handled with the same caution as any other explosive.

IDENTIFYING A BOMB

Once the team locates a bomb, squad members need to figure out what kind of explosive it is. Sometimes, the squad is called in to remove old explosives left behind by the military. In these cases, team members usually know what they're looking for. Other times, they may have no idea what the bomb will look like.

Unfortunately, when people build their own bombs, they can disguise them in many different ways. The bombs may be large or small, and they may be hidden inside other objects. Bomb squads need to continuously learn about different bomb types. They must also think of creative ways to spot new bombs and defuse them.

Recent advances in technology have led to a new type of bomb known as an improvised explosive device (IED). These bombs are usually homemade and look like average, everyday objects. IEDs have been used often in recent wars and terrorist attacks. In response, military bomb technicians have increased their focus on identifying and handling them. IEDs are very difficult to spot because they are often disguised. Bomb technicians must be constantly on alert for anything that looks out of the ordinary.

FACT:
The first U.S. bomb squad in a police department was formed in New York City in 1909.

DEFUSING A BOMB

When the team has located and identified a bomb, team members set to work defusing it. This is often a challenging and stressful process. The team must figure out the safest way to defuse the bomb without getting too close to it or harming anyone in the area.

Sometimes technicians need to defuse the bomb by hand. They wear bomb suits in these cases. Bomb suits can help protect a person in an explosion. However, it doesn't guarantee complete safety. When defusing a bomb manually, a bomb technician may cut the wrong wire and trigger an explosion. This can cause death or injury, even with a bomb suit.

In some cases, it is either too dangerous or impossible to defuse the bomb by hand. In these types of situations, bomb-defusing robots may be used. Bomb technicians can control these robots from a distance. Another option is to **detonate** the bomb in a controlled explosion, if it can be done safely.

detonate—to cause something (such as a bomb) to explode

The Bomb Suit

A bomb suit has many features to protect a bomb technician.

BOMB SUIT FEATURES:

- fire-resistant pants

- trauma plate for the front of the body

- plastic back support to prevent spinal cord injury

- Kevlar jacket with a chest trauma plate

- 15-pound (6.8-kilogram) helmet with lights, a defogger, amplifiers, and a ventilation fan

A bomb expert engineer will use a metal detector to help locate explosive devices to be defused.

Chapter 3

ON THE SCENE

A city police officer is making her rounds during the busy Memorial Day weekend. She spots a car parked and abandoned in a no-parking zone. Getting closer to the vehicle, she notices a strange chemical smell—a sign that a bomb might be present. Peering through the car window, she sees a backpack on the seat with some wires sticking out. In this suspicious situation, it's time to call in the bomb squad.

In this case, locating the bomb isn't difficult. The police officer has already found the suspected bomb. Now, the bomb squad needs to figure out whether there is really a bomb. The squad suspects that the backpack does hold a bomb, probably one that was homemade. It is the bomb squad's job to defuse the bomb before something sets it off.

When the team arrives on the scene, it brings along bomb suits, x-ray machines, bomb blankets, and other tools that might be useful. The technicians confirm the facts that the police officer reported by observing the scene.

When faced with a suspicious package, a bomb squad must handle it with extreme caution until it is defused or deemed safe.

STOPPING THE THREAT

Once the team is reasonably certain a bomb is present, squad members are ready to get to work. Their first job is to **evacuate** all people from the area around the bomb. By clearing the area, people are kept safe from any explosions that might happen.

The team must then decide how to handle the potential bomb. At this point, team members don't know if the backpack actually holds a bomb, what kind of bomb it is, or what could set it off. It is essential for the team to stay calm and make safe decisions.

The squad decides to use a robot to open the car door and transfer the backpack to a special **containment vessel**. After transporting it to a deserted area, squad members detonate the bomb in a controlled explosion. Meanwhile, other members of the team stay behind with bomb-sniffing dogs. They sweep the area in case there are more bombs hidden.

Bomb squads and their canine units protect the capital by detecting any existing explosive devices.

evacuate—to leave a dangerous place and go somewhere safer

containment vessel—a strong container that makes a bomb safer to transport

Bomb Squad in the Capital

At the White House in Washington, D.C., the bomb squad has a unique and busy job. As the capital of the United States, Washington, D.C., receives many bomb threats. When the White House receives a threat, the bomb squad works with the Secret Service to evacuate the building and search for bombs. Fortunately these threats usually do not lead to live bombs. However, the bomb squad still takes every precaution for

Law enforcement and bomb squads were already on the scene at the Boston Marathon and responded immediately after the explosion.

FACT:
The Boston Marathon bombings killed three people and wounded 260 others.

THE BOSTON MARATHON BOMBING

Real-life bomb emergencies can be very difficult to handle. Every call that the bomb squad makes involves risk. It is simply the nature of the job. However, some calls are riskier than others and don't have clear-cut solutions. Bomb technicians may find themselves in situations that are completely new, and they may need to quickly decide what to do.

This was the case on April 15, 2013, the day of the annual Boston Marathon. That morning, the Boston Police Department's bomb squad checked the city's Back Bay neighborhood for explosives. They didn't find anything unusual.

However, two men later planted bombs near the finish line. The bombs were homemade devices, constructed from **pressure cookers** and hidden in backpacks. That afternoon while runners were crossing the finish line, the two bombs exploded. This was a situation the bomb squad never expected. They were still on duty at the marathon, and they quickly jumped into action after the explosions.

pressure cooker–a special pot that is used to cook food quickly by using the pressure of steam

Bomb squads from multiple law enforcement agencies canvassed Boston to ensure that there were no additional explosives.

AN IMMEDIATE RESPONSE

In the chaotic moments following the blasts, no one was certain what was happening. How many people had been hurt? Had anyone been killed? Were there more bombs? As these questions raced through the people's minds, the bomb squad focused on the last question. If there was another bomb, it was the squad's job to find it and **disarm** it before it exploded.

The situation was nothing like training. Sitting among the panicked crowd were rows and rows of abandoned backpacks—all potential bombs. There was no time to use robots or bomb suits. The bomb squad tore into backpacks with knives and their bare hands in search of more bombs. The team members' only goal was to keep the people around them safe.

As the day wore on, the bomb squad performed a more thorough sweep of the whole neighborhood. At one point, they detonated a suspicious bag in a controlled explosion, but it was only a camera bag. Fortunately, there were no more bombs. The Boston Bomb Squad responded to the emergency quickly and kept anyone else from getting hurt.

disarm—to take a bomb apart so it cannot explode

Chapter 4

CLEANING UP

Once a bomb squad has safely defused a bomb, team members must dispose of it properly. The disposal method depends on the type of bomb. Sometimes the components of the bomb are destroyed when the bomb is detonated. Other bombs must be taken apart so nothing can become reconnected and make the bombs live again.

At this point the emergency call is over. However, the bomb technician's job isn't finished. When they're not in the field, bomb squads work on creating emergency plans for the public to use in case of an emergency. Bomb technicians use what they learn on each call to improve these plans.

Bomb technicians must also stay up to date on new kinds of bomb technology. They complete **recertification** courses and training for new skills. They also spend time studying past events to anticipate future emergencies.

Explosive devices are dismantled and disposed of in a safe, professional manner.

recertification—to refresh one's knowledge of a specific subject and be officially certified once again

The Father of the Modern Bomb Squad

One of the founders of modern bomb squad training and practices was Thomas Graham Brodie. He was a police captain and bomb technician. He served in the Miami-Dade Police Department from 1955 to 1983. During that time, Brodie created ingenious new ways to deal with bombs and keep citizens safe. At the same time, he helped start the Hazardous Devices School to train future bomb technicians. Brodie was also a founding member of the International Association of Bomb Technicians and Investigators. He dedicated his time to

BOMB SQUADS IN OUR WORLD

The men and women who serve on bomb squads risk their lives every day to save others from explosive devices. These technicians constantly run toward situations that most people would flee immediately. They bravely find and defuse bombs, where any wrong move could result in serious injury or death.

It takes a lot of specialized training and practice to be a bomb technician. Only trained experts should attempt to defuse bombs. They have the skills and equipment needed to keep them as safe as possible.

Others can do their part by staying alert for suspicious objects and calling 911 if they suspect a bomb. They can feel safe knowing that a highly trained bomb squad is on the way.

Bomb technicians approach and deal with dangerous situations, helping keep civilians safe from explosions.

FACT:
A tool called a pan disrupter shoots high-pressure water at some bombs to prevent them from exploding. The stream of water carefully opens the bomb so that the explosives can be safely removed without the bomb exploding.

GLOSSARY

certify (SUHR-tuh-fy)—to officially recognize a person's abilities and skills

containment vessel (kuhn-TAYN-ment VESS-uhl)—a strong container that makes a bomb safer to transport

defuse (di-FYOOZ)—to remove the part of an explosive that makes it explode

detonate (DE-tuh-nayt)—to cause something (such as a bomb) to explode

disarm (dis-AHRM)—to take a bomb apart so it cannot explode

evacuate (i-VA-kyuh-wayt)—to leave a dangerous place and go somewhere safer

K-9 (KAY-nine)—a dog trained in special skills and used by an official organization such as a bomb squad or police force

observer (uhb-ZUR-vur)—someone who pays close attention to the details of a situation or to his or her surroundings

pressure cooker (PRESH-ur CUK-uhr)—a special pot that is used to cook food quickly by using the pressure of steam

recertification (ree-suhr-tuh-fuh-KAY-shun)—to refresh one's knowledge of a specific subject and be officially certified once again

READ MORE

Gordon, Nick. *Bomb Squad Technician.* Minneapolis: Torque Books, 2012.

Landau, Elaine. *Deadly High-Risk Jobs.* Minneapolis: Lerner, 2013.

Newton, Michael. *Bomb Squad.* Law Enforcement Agencies. New York: Chelsea House Publications, 2010.

Zullo, Allan. *War Heroes: Voices from Iraq.* 10 True Tales. New York: Scholastic, 2009.

CRITICAL THINKING USING THE COMMON CORE

1. What are some reasons a person might make a call to the bomb squad? (Key Ideas and Details)

2. What does someone need to do to become a bomb squad technician? In what types of organizations do bomb squad technicians work? (Key Ideas and Details)

3. What do you think it feels like to work as a bomb squad technician? What might you fear, and how would you face that fear? (Integration of Knowledge and Ideas)

INTERNET SITES

FactHound offers a safe, fun way to find Internet sites related to this book. All of the sites on FactHound have been researched by our staff.

Here's all you do:

Visit *www.facthound.com*

Type in this code: 9781491480281

Check out projects, games and lots more at
www.capstonekids.com

31